THE OFFICIAL
ASTON VILLA
FOOTBALL CLUB

ANNUAL 2022

Compiled by Rob Bishop and Dan Brawn

Special thanks to Gayner Monkton

A Grange Publication

© 2021. Published by Grange Communications Ltd., Edinburgh, under licence from Aston Villa Football Club. Printed in the EU.

Photographs © Neville Williams / Getty Images.

ISBN: 978-1-913578-65-7

EUROPEAN & WORLD HONOURS

EUROPEAN CUP

WINNERS:
1981-82

QUARTER-FINALISTS:
1982-83

EUROPEAN SUPER CUP

WINNERS:
1982-83

WORLD CLUBS CHAMPIONSHIP

RUNNERS-UP:
1982

INTERTOTO CUP

WINNERS:
2001

DOMESTIC HONOURS

PREMIER LEAGUE

RUNNERS-UP:
1992-93

FOOTBALL LEAGUE

CHAMPIONS:
1893-94, 1895-96, 1896-97,
1898-99, 1899-1900,
1909-10, 1980-81

RUNNERS-UP:
1888-89, 1902-03, 1907-08,
1910-11, 1912-13, 1913-14,
1930-31, 1932-33, 1989-90

DIVISION TWO

CHAMPIONS:
1937-38, 1959-60

CHAMPIONSHIP

PLAY-OFF WINNERS:
2019

DIVISION THREE

CHAMPIONS:
1971-72

FA CUP

WINNERS:
1887, 1895, 1897, 1905,
1913, 1920, 1957

RUNNERS-UP:
1892, 1924, 2000, 2015

LEAGUE CUP

WINNERS:
1961, 1975, 1977,
1994, 1996

RUNNERS-UP:
1963, 1971, 2010,
2020

FA YOUTH CUP

WINNERS:
1972, 1980, 2002,
2021

RUNNERS-UP:
2004, 2010

Contents

THE ENTERTAINER

Villa's squad has become increasingly cosmopolitan in recent years, and there are few better examples than Leon Bailey. Born in Jamaica, the tricky winger played in both Belgium and Germany before arriving at Villa Park.

He launched his professional career with Belgian club Genk before making an impact in the Bundesliga, scoring 39 goals in 156 games for Bayer Leverkusen, but he isn't just a goalscorer.

As well as scoring 15 times in league and cup games last season, he also set up 11 goals for team-mates, and he is hoping to continue that trend in claret and blue.

"I like to score but I also like to give assists," he said. "I like to be the one who makes the pass at a decisive moment and not be selfish.

"Whatever situation we are in, I try to adapt. I'm a flair type of person – I like to entertain the fans, to do my tricks, use my speed and make life difficult for defenders."

YOUNG AT HEART!

Ashley Young joined a select club when he returned to Villa Park after an 11-year absence.

The former England midfielder is only the seventh player in the club's history to have more than one spell in claret and blue. Gordon Cowans had three different spells as a Villa player, while Steve Hunt, Andy Gray, Steve Staunton, Andy Blair and James Milner each had two.

Not that Young was thinking about that as he rejoined the club after a decade with Manchester United and a season and a half in Italy with Inter Milan.

"It feels amazing to be back, just like I never left," he said. "I'm delighted to be here, seeing some old faces, being back at the training ground and seeing the facilities. You can see how much the club has evolved since my time.

"When I heard of the interest from Villa, I told my agent to get the deal done. I've still got that winning mentality, the desire and hunger to be successful."

Despite being nearly 36 when he signed for the second time, Ashley is clearly Young at heart!

WELCOME BACK!

Players who have had more than one spell with Villa

STEVE HUNT
1974-77, 1985-88

ANDY GRAY
1975-79, 1985-87

GORDON COWANS
1975-85, 1988-92, 1993-94

ANDY BLAIR
1981-84, 1985-88

STEVE STAUNTON
1991-98, 2000-03

JAMES MILNER
2005-06 (loan), 2008-10

ASHLEY YOUNG
2007-10, 2021-

AXEL TUANZEBE
2018-19 (loan), 2021-

AXEL'S BACK – AGAIN!

In an ideal world, Axel Tuanzebe would be a regular in the Manchester United line-up. But until that happens, he is more than happy to keep joining Villa on loan!

The young defender from the Democratic Republic of Congo is now in his THIRD spell at Villa Park, even though he signed a new contract at Old Trafford just before the start of the season.

He first joined Villa in January 2018, only for injury problems to restrict him to just five games. But after returning for a second loan spell at that start of the 2018-19 season, he made 30 appearances – including the Championship play-off final victory over Derby County at Wembley.

AIMING FOR EUROPE

As we approach the 40th anniversary of the club's 1982 European Cup triumph, Danny Ings is aiming to guide Villa back to Europe – with the help of the supporters.

The 29-year-old striker arrived from Southampton in August, and he made his intentions clear from the outset.

"It's a huge club with a huge reputation and huge expectations from the fans," he said. "This club should be competing for Europe and hopefully I can play my part in achieving that.

"Everywhere I have been in my career, one of the biggest things for me has been to get a bond with the fans as quickly as possible. I've managed that at every club I've been at, and I want the same here."

The England international started his career with Bournemouth and has since played for Burnley and Liverpool before scoring 46 goals in 100 league and cup games for Southampton.

No one will have any complaints if he can achieve a similar ratio after signing a three-year contract with Villa.

ATLANTIC CROSSING!

Most football transfers are conducted close to home. But when Emiliano Buendia became a Villa player, he was over 5,500 miles away, on the other side of the Atlantic!

The Argentine midfielder agreed a move from Norwich City to Villa Park while he was with his international team-mates in Brazil for the 2021 Copa America, even undergoing the obligatory medical in South America.

With his five-year contract signed, sealed and delivered, Buendia was happy to be interviewed by the club's media team via a Zoom link, stressing that he wants to be as successful in claret and blue and he was in the Canaries' yellow and green.

He netted 15 goals last season and set up another 17 as Norwich won promotion to the Premier League, as well as being voted the EFL Championship player of the season.

"It was my best season, in terms of football, goals and assists," he said. "I will work hard to do the same here. The Premier League is the best in the world, so I will be involved with great players.

"It's an amazing step to move to Aston Villa. I like the style and ambition of the club."

OLLIE OLLIE OLLIE!

You might argue that Ollie Watkins was always destined to play for Aston Villa.

Even though he was brought up in Exeter, he made his first visit to Villa Park as a schoolboy, thanks to the former South West Villans supporters' club.

Ollie and his team-mates from his junior team Buckland Athletic travelled with the fans on one of their coaches, enjoying a burger and chips in the Academy building before watching Villa in action.

It was the first time he had watched live Premier League football, so you can imagine the young striker's delight when he finally had the chance to play at such a high level. It was a massive step when he left Championship club Brentford to join Villa, but he was a huge success.

"Getting signed by a Premier League club was a bit surreal," he said. "But I always take everything in my stride and try to enjoy every moment."

Indeed, he finished his first season in English football's top tier as Villa's leading scorer – including a hat-trick in the amazing 7-2 victory over Liverpool – and his impressive performances earned him a call-up to the England team.

His 14-goal total in league games made him only the second English-born player to score so many for Villa in a Premier League season. Julian Joachim also netted 14 in 1998-99.

ENGLAND'S VILLANS

Villa are proud to have served their country down the years – by providing 75 England internationals by the end of last season. Only Tottenham Hotspur have provided more.

It all started back in the Victorian era when Howard Vaughton and Arthur Brown were both in the line-up for a runaway 13-0 victory over Ireland in Belfast in 1882. The Villa duo netted NINE of England's goals between them – five for Vaughton and four for Brown.

Since then, there has been a steady flow of Villa players into the national team, including Gareth Southgate, who is the club's most capped England player with 42 appearances for the national side while at Villa Park.

Ollie Watkins was the latest to make his England debut when he went on as a substitute and scored in a 5-0 victory over San Marino in a World Cup qualifier last March.

Jack Grealish and Tyrone Mings were both in the England squad who reached the European Championship final in July 2021. And Grealish became the first Villa player to represent England in a tournament final when he went on as a substitute in extra-time of the game against Italy at Wembley.

#	Name	Years	Caps
1	ARTHUR BROWN	1882	3
2	HOWARD VAUGHTON	1882-84	5
3	OLIVER WHATELEY	1883	2
4	ALBERT ALLEN	1888	1
5	DENNIS HODGETTS	1888-94	6
6	CHARLIE ATHERSMITH	1892-1900	12
7	JOHN DEVEY	1892-94	2
8	JOHN REYNOLDS	1894-97	5
9	STEVE SMITH	1895	1
10	JIMMY CRABTREE	1896-1902	11
11	HOWARD SPENCER	1897-1905	6
12	FRED WHELDON	1897-98	4
13	ALBERT WILKES	1901-02	5
14	BILLY GEORGE	1902	3
15	BILLY GARRATY	1903	1
16	JOE BACHE	1903-11	7
17	BILLY BRAWN	1904	2
18	ALEX LEAKE	1904-05	5
19	ALBERT HALL	1910	1
20	HARRY HAMPTON	1913-14	4
21	CHARLIE WALLACE	1913-20	3
22	SAM HARDY	1914-20	7
23	FRANK BARSON	1920	1
24	ANDY DUCAT	1920	3
25	BILLY WALKER	1920-32	18
26	BILLY KIRTON	1921	1
27	FRANK MOSS	1921-24	5
28	TOMMY SMART	1921-29	5
29	DICKIE YORK	1922-26	2
30	GEORGE BLACKBURN	1924	1
31	ARTHUR DORRELL	1924-25	4
32	TOMMY MORT	1924-26	3
33	BEN OLNEY	1928	2

Up to August 2021. Goalkeeper Scott Carson was also capped by England while playing for Villa while he was on loan from Liverpool.

34	ERIC HOUGHTON	1930-31	7
35	JOE TATE	1931-32	3
36	TOM 'PONGO' WARING	1931-32	5
37	GEORGE BROWN	1932	1
38	RONNIE STARLING	1933-37	1
39	JOE BERESFORD	1934	1
40	TOMMY GARDNER	1934-35	2
41	FRANK BROOME	1938-39	7
42	EDDIE LOWE	1947	3
43	TOMMY THOMPSON	1951	1
44	GERRY HITCHENS	1961	3
45	BRIAN LITTLE	1975	1
46	JOHN GIDMAN	1977	1
47	TONY MORLEY	1981-82	6
48	PETER WITHE	1981-84	11
49	NIGEL SPINK	1983	1
50	GORDON COWANS	1983-90	8
51	STEVE HODGE	1986	11
52	DAVID PLATT	1989	22
53	TONY DALEY	1991-92	7
54	EARL BARRETT	1993	2
55	KEVIN RICHARDSON	1994	1
56	GARETH SOUTHGATE	1995-02	42
57	UGO EHIOGU	1996	1
58	STAN COLLYMORE	1997	1
59	DION DUBLIN	1998	1
60	LEE HENDRIE	1998	1
61	PAUL MERSON	1998	1
62	GARETH BARRY	2000-09	29
63	DAVID JAMES	2001	3
64	DARIUS VASSELL	2002-04	22
65	ASHLEY YOUNG	2007-08	15
66	GABBY AGBONLAHOR	2008-09	3
67	EMILE HESKEY	2009-10	12
68	JAMES MILNER	2008-10	12
69	STEPHEN WARNOCK	2010	1
70	DARREN BENT	2011	6
71	STEWART DOWNING	2011	4
72	FABIAN DELPH	2014-15	6
73	TYRONE MINGS	2019-	13
74	JACK GREALISH	2020-21	12
75	OLLIE WATKINS	2021-	3

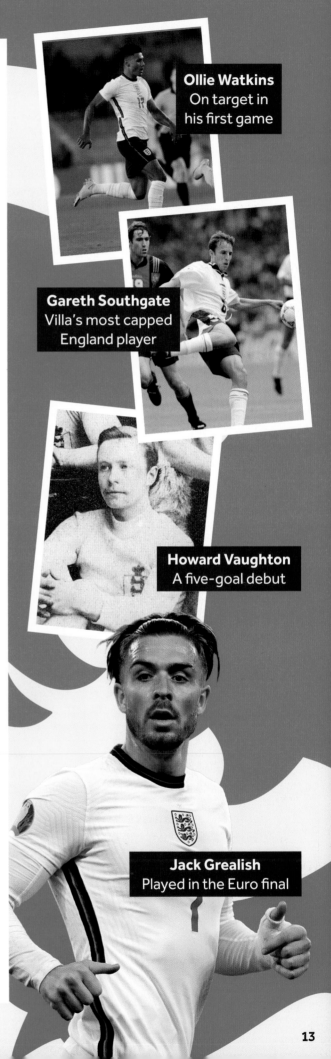

Ollie Watkins
On target in his first game

Gareth Southgate
Villa's most capped England player

Howard Vaughton
A five-goal debut

Jack Grealish
Played in the Euro final

Player Managers

Here are six Villa managers who have something in common – they were also on the club's books as players in their younger days.

Can you re-arrange the order in which they appear to match the order in which they were in charge at Villa Park?

And do you know which one never played for Villa's first team?

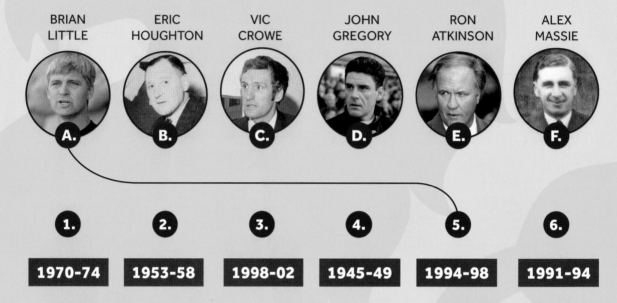

BRIAN LITTLE   ERIC HOUGHTON   VIC CROWE   JOHN GREGORY   RON ATKINSON   ALEX MASSIE

A.   B.   C.   D.   E.   F.

1.   2.   3.   4.   5.   6.

1970-74   1953-58   1998-02   1945-49   1994-98   1991-94

Spot the Ball

Answers on page 60

A FRENCH LESSON

If your family enjoy holidays in France, you might have heard the expression "taking French Leave."

Well, our friends across the Channel have a similar phrase for a French person who spends time in this country – and it made a perfect headline when Morgan Sanson joined Villa.

The popular sports newspaper L'Equipe's story about the midfielder's transfer from Olympique Marseille was headlined: "Il file a l'Anglaise" which essentially means "he takes English Leave"!

Sanson arrived at Villa Park during the January 2021 transfer window after four years at the Stade Velodrome in which he established himself as one of the best midfielders in Ligue 1.

He also experienced Champions League football, so it speaks volumes for Villa's reputation that he jumped at the chance to move to the West Midlands.

"It has been my dream to play in the Premier League since I was a boy," he said. "I am a warrior and I like it when players run and work hard for the team. But Villa also play good football."

Sanson file à l'anglaise

Le milieu de l'OM va rejoindre Aston Villa pour un peu moins de 16 M€. Longoria, qui a un budget d'une dizaine de millions d'euros, cherche un profil plus offensif pour renforcer ce secteur

VINCENT GARCIA
et MATHIEU GRÉGOIRE

15

2021/22 SQUAD

EMILIANO
MARTINEZ

GOALKEEPER

Born: MAR DEL PLATA, ANGENTINA

D.O.B.: 02.09.92

Signed: SEPT 2020

Previous club: ARSENAL

JED
STEER

Born: NORWICH

D.O.B.: 23.09.92

Signed: JULY 2013

Previous club:
NORWICH CITY

GOALKEEPER

LOVRE
KALINIC

Born: SPLIT, CROATIA

D.O.B.: 03.04.90

Signed: JAN 2019

Previous club: GENT

ON LOAN

GOALKEEPER

TYRONE
MINGS

Born: BATH
D.O.B.: 13.03.93
Signed: JULY 2019
Previous club:
BOURNEMOUTH

DEFENDER

MATT
TARGETT

Born: EASTLEIGH
D.O.B.: 18.09.95
Signed: JUNE 2019
Previous club:
SOUTHAMPTON

DEFENDER

MATTY
CASH

DEFENDER

Born: SLOUGH
D.O.B.: 07.08.97
Signed: SEPT 2020
Previous club:
NOTTINGHAM FOREST

FREDERIC
GUILBERT

Born: VALOGNES,
FRANCE
D.O.B.: 24.12.94
Signed: JAN2019
Previous club: CAEN

ON LOAN

DEFENDER

EZRI
KONSA

Born: **NEWHAM**

D.O.B.: **23.10.97**

Signed: **JULY 2019**

Previous club:
BRENTFORD

DEFENDER

ASHLEY
YOUNG

DEFENDER

Born: **STEVENAGE**

D.O.B.: **09.07.85**

Signed: **JULY 2021**

Previous club:
INTER MILAN

AXEL
TUANZEBE

Born: **BUNIA, DR CONGO**

D.O.B.: **14.11.97**

Signed: **AUG 2021**

Previous club:
MANCHESTER UTD.

DEFENDER

KORTNEY
HAUSE

Born: **GOODMAYES**

D.O.B.: **16.07.95**

Signed: **JUNE 2019**

Previous club: **WOLVES**

DEFENDER

AVFC

DOUGLAS
LUIZ

Born: RIO DE JANEIRO, BRAZIL
D.O.B.: 09.05.98
Signed: JULY 2019
Previous club: MAN CITY

MIDFIELDER

EMILIANO
BUENDIA

Born: MAR DEL PLATA, ARENGTINA
D.O.B.: 25.12.96
Signed: JULY 2021
Previous club: NORWICH CITY

MIDFIELDER

MARVELOUS
NAKAMBA

Born: ZIMBABWE
D.O.B.: 19.01.94
Signed: AUG 2019
Previous club: CLUB BRUGGE

MIDFIELDER

AVFC

MORGAN
SANSON

Born: SAINT-DOULCHARD, FRANCE
D.O.B.: 18.08.94
Signed: JAN 2021
Previous club: MARSEILLE

MIDFIELDER

ANWAR
EL GHAZI

MIDFIELDER

Born: BARENDRECHT
D.O.B.: 03.05.95
Signed: AUG 2018
Previous club: LILLE OSC

CONOR
HOURIHANE

Born: BANDON, IRELAND
D.O.B.: 02.02.91
Signed: JAN 2017
Previous club: BARNSLEY

ON LOAN

MIDFIELDER

TREZEGUET

Born: KARF EL SHEIK, EGYPT
D.O.B.: 01.10.94
Signed: JULY 2019
Previous club: KASIMPASA

MIDFIELDER

JADEN
PHILOGENE-BIDACE

MIDFIELDER

Born: LONDON
D.O.B.: 08.02.02
Signed: ACADEMY GRADUATE

JOHN
McGINN

Born: GLASGOW
D.O.B.: 18.10.94
Signed: AUG 2018
Previous club: HIBERNIAN

MIDFIELDER

CARNEY
CHUKWUEMEKA

Born: AUSTRIA
D.O.B.: 20.10.03
Signed: ACAMEDY GRADUATE

MIDFIELDER

LEON
BAILEY

Born: KINGSTON, JAMAICA

D.O.B.: 09.08.97

Signed: AUG 2021

Previous club: BAYER LEVERKUSEN

MIDFIELDER

BERTRAND
TRAORE

Born: BOBO-DIOULASSO, BURKINA FASO

D.O.B.: 06.09.95

Signed: SEPT2020

Previous club: LYON

MIDFIELDER

JACOB
RAMSEY

Born: BIRMINGHAM,

D.O.B.: 28.05.01

Signed:ACADEMY GRADUATE

MIDFIELDER

OLLIE
WATKINS

STRIKER

Born: TORQUAY

D.O.B.: 30.12.95

Signed: SEPT 2020

Previous club: BRENTFORD

AVFC

KEINAN
DAVIS

Born: STEVENAGE
D.O.B.: 13.02.98
Signed: DEC 2015
Previous club:
BIGGLESWADE TOWN

STRIKER

DANNY
INGS

STRIKER

Born: WINCHESTER
D.O.B.: 23.07.92
Signed: AUG 2021
Previous club:
SOUTHAMPTON

WESLEY
MORAES

Born: JUIZ DE FORA,
BRAZIL
D.O.B.: 26.11.96
Signed: JULY 2019
Previous club:
CLUB BRUGGE

ON LOAN

STRIKER

Do you know Ezri Konsa

1. Where was Ezri born? Was it:

☐ A. LONDON

☐ B. LEICESTER

☐ C. LINCOLN

2. With which club did he begin his professional career?

☐ A. CARDIFF CITY

☐ B. COVENTRY CITY

☐ C. CHARLTON ATHLETIC

3. From which club did he join Villa in 2019?

☐ A. BOURNEMOUTH

☐ B. BRIGHTON

☐ C. BRENTFORD

4. Ezri scored after just four minutes of his Villa debut, in a League Cup tie. Who were our opponents?

☐ A. CARLISLE UNITED

☐ B. CREWE ALEXANDRA

☐ C. CHELSEA

5. His first Premier League goal helped Villa to avoid relegation in 2020. Can you remember our opponents in that 1-1 draw?

☐ A. EVERTON

☐ B. NEWCASTLE UNITED

☐ C. WEST HAM

Answers on page 61

AVFC

KONSA
KONSA
KONSA
KONSA
KONSA

The French Connection

Until the arrival of Didier Six in 1984, Villa had never had a French player, and it was still a rarity when the flamboyant David Ginola signed from Newcastle United in 2000.

But over the past decade or so, French signings have been far more frequent, so it was no great surprise when Morgan Sanson arrived in January 2021.

See if you can find 11 French Villans in this wordsearch. Some of the names go across the grid, some go up and down – and one is diagonal. The names you are looking for are listed below.

S	A	N	S	O	N	A	E	G	L
Y	M	B	M	R	X	J	G	H	N
L	A	U	C	W	D	S	I	X	A
F	V	B	E	R	S	O	N	Q	O
C	I	S	S	O	K	H	O	S	G
H	J	E	Y	N	K	P	L	B	L
I	V	R	D	C	T	W	A	E	I
G	U	I	L	B	E	R	T	Y	A
O	K	P	A	Y	L	Z	B	E	W
J	A	D	A	K	O	D	J	I	A

Morgan **SANSON**   Habib **BEYE**   Jonathan **KODJIA**

Jordan **AMAVI**   Aly **CISSOKHO**   Robert **PIRES**

Jordan **AYEW**   David **GINOLA**   Didier **SIX**

Mathieu **BERSON**   Frederic **GUILBERT**

Answers on page 61

SEVENTH HEAVEN

Of all the unexpected results in Villa's history, the one on the first weekend of October 2020 was surely the most unlikely of them all:

Aston Villa 7 Liverpool 2!

How on earth did Dean Smith's side, who had narrowly escaped relegation the previous season, record such an emphatic victory over the team who had been runaway winners of the Premier League?

The mighty Merseysiders arrived at Villa Park after starting the defence of their title with three straight wins. But a positive approach from the home side reaped incredible rewards. Quite simply, Smith's slick operators looked capable of scoring every time they attacked.

The only previous time Villa had scored seven in the Premier League was a quarter of a century earlier, against Wimbledon in 1995. But on a crazy night in 2020 we witnessed the almost unbelievable demolition of genuine football aristocrats.

Just four minutes had elapsed when a mistake by Liverpool keeper Adrian enabled Jack Grealish to set up record signing Ollie Watkins for his first goal at this level. That one was a simple tap-in, but Watkins' second was a sight to behold as he moved in to Grealish's astute through ball, cut inside from the left and sent a rising right-foot drive into the far corner.

Mo Salah reduced the deficit, but by half-time John McGinn had fired home a long-range drive and Watkins had completed his hat-trick with a close-range header from Trezeguet's cross.

On-loan midfielder Ross Barkley marked his debut by taking the score to 5-1 following another Grealish assist, and although Salah reduced the deficit with a cool finish, Villa were far from finished.

Having created so many other openings, Grealish got in on the scoring act, first with a shot which deflected in off Fabinho and then a cheeky chip past the advancing Adrian following McGinn's magnificent pass.

It was a game we will be talking about for years to come!

AVFC 7-2 LIVERPOOL

adi.tv

TRAINING FOR 50 YEARS!

There's much more to football than 90 minutes of action on match day.

Throughout the week, Villa's players are hard at work at Bodymoor Heath, which has been the club's training ground for over half a century.

The original Bodymoor Heath training ground was officially opened on 10th November 1971, when the unveiling was performed by Bert Bond, Villa's stadium manager and former groundsman, in recognition of his 30 years' service to the club.

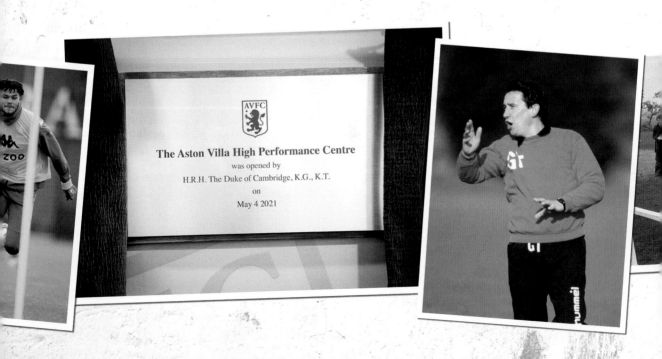

Before that, Villa had been without satisfactory training facilities since the mid-1960s, when the club sold their old training ground in Trinity Road, not far from Villa Park.

The Bodymoor site provided the perfect solution, comprising nearly 20 acres of grassland which the club purchased from a farmer called Mr Davies and then redeveloped at a cost of £65,000.

Apart from the addition of a large "barn" which was used as a gym, the old building was largely unaltered before its demolition.

In May 2007, it was replaced by a new £13 million state-of-the-art complex, located a few hundred yards away. Martin O'Neill, then Villa's manager, performed the official opening, assisted by skipper Gareth Barry and Villa's European Cup-winning captain Dennis Mortimer.

In 2019, a 500-seat mini-stadium was built at Bodymoor for the staging of under-23 home games. And in May 2021, HRH The Duke of Cambridge – a keen Villa supporter – officially opened Bodymoor's new High Performance Centre.

Spot the Difference

There are EIGHT differences between these two pictures. Can you find them all?

Answers on page 61

THE LONGEST NAME!

Jaden Philogene-Bidace made an unusual piece of club history when he went on as a late substitute in Villa's 2-1 victory at Tottenham Hotspur at the end of last season.

The London-born winger's debut meant he became the player with the longest surname ever to play for Villa's first team!

Jaden's double-barrel name runs to 15 letters – one more than the previous longest, Corey Blackett-Taylor, who made one substitute appearance in 2017 and William Barnie-Adshead, an amateur defender who played two games in 1922.

There have been a few lengthy Villa surnames, including John Sleeuwenhoek in the 1960s, Eric Djemba-Djemba, who joined Villa from Manchester United in January 2005 and Rushian Hepburn-Murphy, who became the club's youngest Premier League player in 2015.

But 19-year-old Philogene-Bidace is longer than them all – and another youngster with a lengthy name made his debut in the same match.

Midfielder Carney Chukwuemeka also made his debut at Tottenham, and the 17-year-old almost scored with a low shot which hit the foot of the post.

SEASON
2020/21
REVIEW

KEINAN DAVIS

RESULTS

Sept 17
Burton Albion (CC) A   3-1
Watkins, Grealish, Davis

Sept 21
Sheffield United H   1-0
Konsa

Sept 24
Bristol City (CC) A   3-0
El Ghazi, Traore, Watkins

Sept 28
Fulham A   3-0
Grealish, Hourihane, Mings

Dean Smith's men make a flying start to the campaign, taking maximum points from their first two Premier League games as well as progressing to the fourth round of the Carabao Cup.

Unusually, the season gets under way with a cup tie, and Villa are behind inside two minutes against Burton Albion at the Pirelli Stadium. But new boy Ollie Watkins marks his debut by cancelling out the Brewers' early lead before late goals from Jack Grealish and Keinan Davis clinch victory.

Bertrand Traore follows Watkins' example by scoring on his debut in the third round, a magnificent volley in a 3-0 win over Bristol City at Ashton Gate.

There are two heroes in the opening Premier League game against Sheffield United at Villa Park. New keeper Emi Martinez saves a penalty in the first half before defender Ezri Konsa secures a winning start with a well-placed header after Tyrone Mings flicks on Matt Targett's corner.

A fourth-minute Grealish goal provides the best possible start against newly-promoted Fulham at Craven Cottage, Villa going on to enjoy a comfortable win with further strikes from Conor Hourihane and Mings.

7-2

OCTOBER

Amazing, incredible, sensational, unbelievable – take your pick to describe Villa's 7-2 victory over champions Liverpool at Villa Park. Ollie Watkins helps himself to a perfect hat-trick – a left-foot shot, a right-foot shot and a header – while skipper Jack Grealish is on target twice. Ross Barkley, on loan from Chelsea, marks his debut with a goal, while John McGinn also gets his name on the scoresheet.

It's the first time for 58 years that Villa have started the season with three consecutive league wins – and they achieve another milestone in the following game. A last-minute Ross Barkley goal clinches a 1-0 win against Leicester City at the King Power makes it four in a row. The last time that happened was in 1930.

Unfortunately, the prospect of a club record five-match winning start is wrecked by Patrick Bamford's second-half hat-trick for Leeds United as Villa miss the chance to go top of the table for the first time since 2001.

RESULTS

Oct 1
Stoke City (CC) H   0-1

Oct 4
Liverpool H   7-2
Watkins 3, Grealish 2,
McGinn, Barkley

Oct 15
Leicester City A   1-0
Barkley

Oct 24
Leeds United H   0-3

RESULTS

Nov 2
Southampton H   **3-4**
Mings, Watkins (pen) Grealish

Nov 8
Arsenal A   **3-0**
Saka og, Watkins 2

Nov 21
Brighton H   **1-2**
Konsa

Nov 28
West Ham United A   **1-2**
Grealish

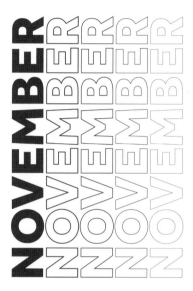

NOVEMBER
NOVEMBER
NOVEMBER
NOVEMBER
NOVEMBER
NOVEMBER
NOVEMBER

After a demoralising second-half against Leeds, Villa seem to be still in shock as they go three-down by half-time against Southampton at Villa Park. The visitors score again by the hour mark before goals from Tyrone Mings, Ollie Watkins and Jack Grealish at least make the scoreline more respectable.

If that result is a setback, though, Dean Smith's side bounce back with a magnificent 3-0 victory over Arsenal at the Emirates Stadium, where Ollie Watkins scores two goals in the space of three second-half minutes to add to Bukayo Saka's own goal. The win could have been even more emphatic, John McGinn having an effort disallowed following a four-minute VAR review and Jack Grealish seeing a shot cleared off the line.

There's further VAR controversy in back-to-back defeats at the hands of Brighton and West Ham, Villa being denied a penalty against the Seagulls and an Ollie Watkins equaliser against the Hammers.

A battling performance, plus some brilliant saves from Emi Martinez , enable Villa to emerge with all three points against Wolves, thanks to Anwar El Ghazi's late penalty after John McGinn is brought down.

Despite being well on top, Villa settle for a point in a goalless home draw against Burnley. But they are back to winning ways with a 3-0 success over West Bromwich Albion at The Hawthorns, where El Ghazi makes the breakthrough with an early goal and completes the scoring from the penalty spot. In between times, Bertrand Traore strokes home a sublime shot for his first Premier League goal for the club.

Traore is on target again on Boxing Day, opening the scoring against Crystal Palace in the fifth minute. Despite having Tyrone Mings sent off, Villa go on to win 3-0 with a Kortney Hause header and a stunning shot from El Ghazi, who makes it five in as many games with the equaliser against Chelsea at Stamford Bridge.

RESULTS

Dec 12
Wolves A   **1-0**
El Ghazi (pen)

Dec 17
Burnley H   **0-0**

Dec 20
West Bromwich Albion A   **3-0**
El Ghazi 2 (1 pen) Traore

Dec 26
Crystal Palace H   **3-0**
Traore, Hause, El Ghazi

Dec 28
Chelsea A   **1-1**
El Ghazi

JANUARY

JANUARY
JANUARY
JANUARY
JANUARY

RESULTS

Jan 1
Manchester United A   1-2
Traore

Jan 8
Liverpool (FAC 3) H   1-4
Barry

Jan 20
Manchester City A   0-2

Jan 23
Newcastle United H   2-0
Watkins, Traore

Jan 27
Burnley A   2-3
Watkins, Grealish

Jan 30
Southampton A   1-0
Barkley

The new year gets off to the worst possible start – a defeat by Manchester United at Old Trafford followed by an outbreak of Covid-19 at the Bodymoor Heath training complex.

With several first-team players and staff affected, Villa are forced to field a team of under-23 and under-18 players for the third-round FA Cup tie at home to Liverpool. The youngsters give a good account of themselves, even equalising with a superb Louie Barry goal, before making their exit.

Two Premier League home games are subsequently postponed before Villa return to action with mixed fortunes. They suffer further defeats at Manchester City and Burnley – despite leading twice at Turf Moor – but are convincing winners at home to Newcastle United before Ross Barkley's superb header from a Jack Grealish cross clinches a narrow victory over Southampton at St Mary's.

RESULTS

Feb 3
West Ham United H   1-3
Watkins

Feb 6
Arsenal H   1-0
Watkins

Feb 13
Brighton A   0-0

Feb 20
Leicester City H   1-2
Traore

Feb 27
Leeds United A   1-0
El Ghazi

Ollie Watkins takes his goal haul to 12 – ten of them in the Premier League – by scoring in back-to-back home games against West Ham and Arsenal.

His goal against the Hammers isn't enough to prevent a 3-1 defeat, but three days later he strikes after just 73 seconds to secure a 1-0 success over the Gunners.

The brilliant Emi Martinez keeps his 12th clean sheet of the season to earn a goalless draw against Brighton at the Amex Stadium, although Bertrand Traore's goal just after half-time isn't enough to prevent a 2-1 home defeat by Leicester City.

But Villa return to winning ways as Anwar El Ghazi's early strike at Elland Road secures a 1-0 verdict against Leeds United.

RESULTS

March 3
Sheffield United A   0-1

March 6
Wolves H   0-0

March 13
Newcastle United A   1-1
Clark (og)

March 21
Tottenham Hotspur H   0-2

MARCH
MARCH
MARCH
MARCH
MARCH

All Villa have to show for a depressing month is one point and one goal – and even that is an own goal.

After slipping to a single-goal defeat to bottom-of-the-table Sheffield United at Bramall Lane, Dean Smith's side have to settle for a goalless draw at home to Wolves, with Ollie Watkins and Ezri Konsa both firing against the bar during the first half.

Hitting the target has become a problem for Dean Smith's side. Even when they take an 86th-minute lead against Newcastle United at St James' Park, it's courtesy of an own goal from former Villan Ciaran Clark – and victory is denied when Jamaal Lascelles heads a stoppage-time equaliser.

To complete a miserable March, the team are again off form as they slip to a home defeat at the hands of Tottenham Hotspur.

RESULTS

April 3
Fulham H   3-1
Trezeguet 2, Watkins

April 10
Liverpool A   1-2
Watkins

April 17
Manchester City H   1-2
McGinn

April 24
West Bromwich Albion H   2-2
El Ghazi pen, Davis

Trezeguet assumes the role of super sub against Fulham. With Villa trailing to an Aleksandar Mitrovic goal, the Egyptian midfielder replaces Anwar El Ghazi – and goes on to score twice in a 3-1 victory. Ollie Watkins completes the scoring with his 11th Premier League goal of the season.

Watkins is on target again the following weekend, opening the scoring at Anfield, only for Liverpool to emerge winners with goals from Mohamed Salah and Trent Alexander-Arnold.

When John McGinn scores Villa's second-fastest Premier League goal after just 20 seconds, hopes are raised of a surprise home win over Manchester City, only for the champions-elect to hit back through Phil Foden and Rodrigo before half-time.

Villa look destined for a third straight defeat when they trail West Bromwich Albion going into stoppage time, despite having taken an early lead through an Anwar El Ghazi penalty. But sub Keinan Davis rescues a point as he takes advantage of hesitancy in the Baggies defence to claim his first Premier League goal.

MAY MAY MAY MAY MAY

RESULTS

May 1
Everton A   2-1
Watkins, El Ghazi

May 9
Manchester United H   1-3
Traore

May 13
Everton H   0-0

May 16
Crystal Palace A   2-3
McGinn, El Ghazi

May 19
Tottenham Hotspur A   2-1
Reguilon (og), Watkins

May 23
Chelsea H   2-1
Traore, El Ghazi pen

Villa start the final month of the season by climbing to ninth in the table. Anwar El Ghazi hits a superb winner ten minutes from the end at Everton after Ollie Watkins' early strike is cancelled out by a Dominic Calvert-Lewin header.

Bertrand Traore's superb shot into the top corner isn't enough to prevent a home defeat by Manchester United and Villa again struggle at home in a goalless draw against Everton.

They lead twice, through John McGinn and El Ghazi, only to lose 3-2 against Crystal Palace, but follow up with an impressive win at Tottenham. Despite conceding an early goal, Villa draw level with a spectacular own goal from Sergio Reguilon before Ollie Watkins hits the winner.

The season ends on a high note. With 10,000 supporters inside Villa Park for the final game, goals from Traore and Anwar El Ghazi – a penalty after Traore is fouled in the area – clinch a memorable victory over fourth-placed Chelsea.

AWESOME FOUR-SOMES!

Villa's four-match winning start to the 2020-21 campaign left other clubs in no doubt that the boys in claret and blue really meant business in their second season back in the Premier League.

It was only the fifth occasion that Villa have made such a flying start – and the last time it had happened was 90 years earlier!

That was in 1930-31, the amazing season when the team's cavalier approach brought them an incredible 128 league goals, including 49 for Tom "Pongo" Waring.

Villa's total is a record which no other club have ever surpassed, while Pongo's impressive haul (he also scored one in the FA Cup) is the highest number of goals for a Villa player in a single season.

Before that, Villa also kicked off with four wins in 1891, 1897 and 1900, so the class of 2020 have every reason to feel proud of their achievement.

2020-21

Sheffield United	H	1-0
Fulham	A	3-0
Liverpool	H	7-2
Leicester City	A	1-0

1891-92

Blackburn Rovers	H	5-1
West Bromwich Albion	H	5-1
Preston North End	A	1-0
Sunderland	H	5-1

1897-98

Sheffield Wednesday	H	5-2
West Bromwich Albion	H	4-3
Notts County	A	3-2
Bury	H	3-1

1900-01

Stoke	H	2-0
Preston North End	H	4-0
West Bromwich Albion	A	1-0
Sunderland	H	1-0

1930-31

Manchester United	A	4-3
Sheffield Wednesday	H	2-0
West Ham	H	6-1
Grimsby Town	A	2-1

FIRST GOALS

OLLIE WATKINS

v Burton A. (a) 3-1

The new boy marks his debut with the equaliser in a second-round Carabao Cup tie at the Pirelli Stadium, tapping in from close range following Jack Grealish's precise pass and Neil Taylor's low cross.

ROSS BARKLEY

v Liverpool (h) 7-2

Yet another debut goal, this time in the Premier League, as the loan signing accepts a short pass from Jack Grealish before his left-foot shot from the edge of the penalty area takes a slight deflection into the top corner.

BERTRAND TRAORE

v Bristol City (a) 3-0

A sublime side-footed angled volley at Ashton Gate, following a lofted pass from Jacob Ramsey, is the highlight of an emphatic Villa victory in the third round of the Carabao Cup.

LOUIE BARRY

v Liverpool (h) 1-4

Moving on to Callum Rowe's superb through ball, Barry strokes a sublime low shot beyond the advancing keeper and into the far corner.

...AND THE DEBUT BOYS

OLLIE WATKINS	Burton Albion (CC)	A	3-1
EMILIANO MARTINEZ	Sheffield United	H	1-0
MATTY CASH	Sheffield United	H	1-0
BERTRAND TRAORE	Bristol City (CC)	A	3-0
ROSS BARKLEY	Liverpool	H	7-2
MORGAN SANSON	West Ham	H	1-3
CARNEY CHUKWUEMEKA	Tottenham Hotspur	A	2-1
JADEN PHILOGENE-BIDACE	Tottenham Hotspur	A	2-1

In addition, 16 youngsters made their first-team debuts when Villa were forced to field a team of inexperienced players in the third-round FA Cup tie against Liverpool. Check them out on pages 46 and 47.

Find the full-backs

Matty Cash became the latest in a long line of classy full-backs when he joined Villa from Nottingham Forest.

Using his name, see how many other quality right-backs and left-backs you can find. To help you out, we have provided the players' first names, the first initial of their surnames and the years they were at Villa Park.

1. **John G** _ _ _ _ _   (1972-1980)

2. **Gary C** _ _ _ _ _ _   (1994-1999)

3. **Steve S** _ _ _ _ _ _ _ _ (1991-1998 & 2000-2003)

4. **Charlie A** _ _ _ _ _   (1960-1976)

5. **Mark D** _ _ _ _ _ _   (1998-2006)

6. **Chris P** _ _ _ _   (1988-1992)

7. **Kenny S** _ _ _ _   (1978-1983)

8. **Colin G** _ _ _ _ _   (1978-1986)

9. **Alan W** _ _ _ _ _ _   (1994-2003)

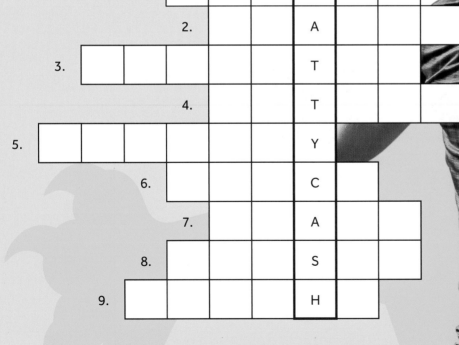

1. M
2. A
3. T
4. T
5. Y
6. C
7. A
8. S
9. H

Answers on page 60

KEEP IT CLEAN!

Footballers don't usually leave a club shortly after winning an FA cup medal, but that is exactly what Emiliano Martinez did.

The Argentine keeper helped Arsenal to a 2-1 victory in the final on the first day of August 2020 and was back at Wembley at the end of the month as the Gunners beat Liverpool on penalties in the Community Shield – the annual game between the Premier League champions and the Cup winners.

But by the middle of September he was a Villa player, marking his debut with a penalty save as Dean Smith's men beat Sheffield United 1-0. And he went on to keep 15 clean sheets, equalling Brad Friedel's Premier League club record from 2009-10.

That debut against the Blades will always be special to him. As he pointed out: "When you get a win, a clean sheet and a penalty save all in one game, it's the same feeling as when you get a hat-trick!"

Emi had been with the Gunners for over a decade but had made a total of just 38 appearances. He repeated that figure in just one season with Villa.

MARK'S MINORS!

Villa's youngest-ever line-up has been a topic for debate down the decades, with the Mercer's Minors teams of the early 1960s the most obvious candidates. Until 2021, that was.

Now we have a definitive answer. On Friday 8th January, the club were forced to field a starting line-up with an average age of under 20 for the third-round FA Cup tie at home to Liverpool.

With the first-team squad self-isolating because of an outbreak of Covid-19, Villa had no option but to use youth players for the game against the mighty Merseysiders.

At 21 years and four months, left-back Callum Rowe was the oldest member of the side. Dutch midfielder Lamare Bogarde was the youngest, at 16 years and 11 months.

Under-23 coach Mark Delaney took charge of the team, and the former Villa and Wales right-back watched proudly from the touchline at Villa Park as his youngsters produced an admirable performance.

Despite falling behind to a Sadio Mane goal inside four minutes, Mark's Minors equalised just before half-time with a sublime finish from Louie Barry, who couldn't disguise his elation as he raced to share the moment with Villa's substitutes.

It wasn't until the hour mark, when Jurgen Klopp's side scored three times in six minutes through Georginio Wijnaldum, Mane and Mo Salah, that the visitors were assured of their passage to the fourth round.

Despite the 4-1 scoreline the Villa kids had every reason to feel proud of themselves on a night they wrote themselves into football history.

Aston Villa 1
Liverpool 4

FA Cup 3rd Round
08 January 2021

AKOS ONODI
(20/09/2001)

JAKE WALKER
(20/09/2001)

DOMINIC REVAN
(19/09/2000)

MUNGO BRIDGE
(12/09/2000)

CALLUM ROWE
(02/09/1999)

KAINE KESLER
(23/10/2002)

ARJAN RAIKHY
(20/10/2002)

MAMADOU SYLLA
(12/08/2002)

LAMARE BOGARDE
(03/02/2004)

HAYDEN LINDLEY
(02/09/2002)

LOUIE BARRY
(21/06/2003)

YOUNGER STILL!

Despite being the youngest line-up to represent Villa's first team, none of the lads who faced Liverpool could claim to be the youngest player in the club's history.

That distinction belongs to Jimmy Brown, who was 15 years and 349 days when he made his debut at Bolton in September 1969.

Villa's youngest-ever scorer was Walter Hazelden, who was 16 years and 269 days when he netted against West Bromwich Albion at The Hawthorns in November 1957.

THE KIDS ARE ALL RIGHT!

It really was an unforgettable season at Villa Park – and not just for the first team.

Just over 24 hours after Dean Smith's men signed off with a Premier League victory over Chelsea, the club's under-18s celebrated an FA Youth Cup triumph.

The youngsters beat Liverpool 2-1 in the final, thanks to two goals in the first 11 minutes. Ben Chrisene opened the scoring before Brad Young netted with a cheeky penalty.

Although the Merseysiders reduced the deficit on 73 minutes, Villa held firm to lift the trophy for the fourth time in the club's history, having also won it in 1972, 1980 and 2002.

The Class of 2021 started with a 4-3 win at Reading, followed by 3-0 win over Brighton and a 9-0 romp against Burton Albion.

They then won 6-1 at Newcastle before beating neighbours West Brom 4-1 in the semi-final.

Name on the shirt

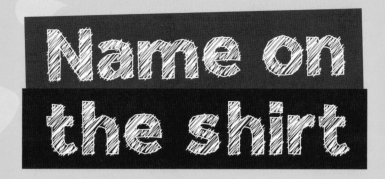

Villa's kit manager isn't happy – someone has mixed up the letters of the players' names on the back of their shirts. Look carefully at these anagrams to reveal the players in question.

ASK TWIN
1

SING
2

CHAS
3

SIGN M
4

NO ASK
5

A RETRO
6

IV SAD
7

SMEARY
8

GREAT TT
9

CN MING
10

ANN SOS
11

GETTERUZE
12

Answers on page 61

AVFC

JOIN THE PRIDE

2021/22 MEMBERSHIP

Become Part of the Pride

Our junior fans can get access to some fantastic benefits, including:

- Priority ticket access
- 20% Soccer school discount*
- Entry into the matchday mascot competition ballot*
- Exclusive members events
- Birthday and Christmas card
- Exclusive competitions
- Member only content
- Games and downloads
- Plus much, much more...

Villans (12-17)

Cubs (3-11)

Little Villans (0-2)

TO LEARN MORE VISIT MEMBERSHIP.AVFC.CO.UK

GETTING SHIRTY

Some football supporters collect programmes, others prefer badges, postcards or various other claret-and-blue memorabilia.

Dave Hitchman's passion is match-worn shirts, and he has over 300 which have been worn by Villa players down the years.

Here's a selection from Dave's impressive collection, and you can check out lots more by visiting his website – www.astonvillashirts.co.uk

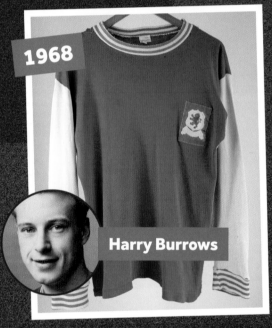

1968

Harry Burrows

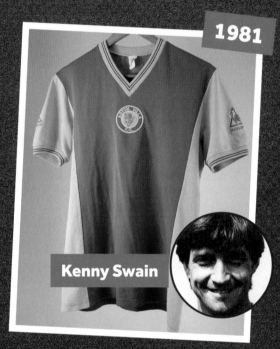

1981

Kenny Swain

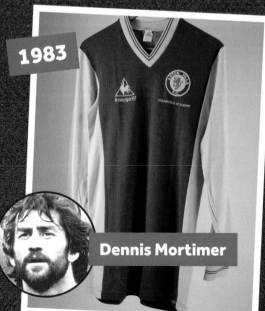

1983

Dennis Mortimer

1991

Paul McGrath

1992

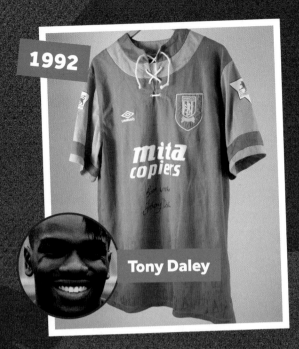

Tony Daley

1994

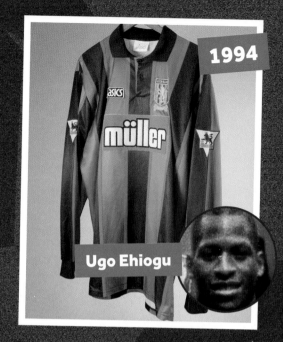

Ugo Ehiogu

1997

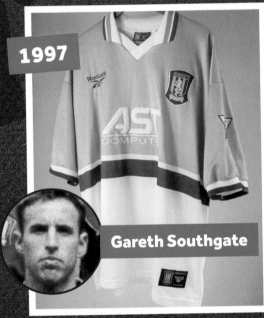

Gareth Southgate

2002

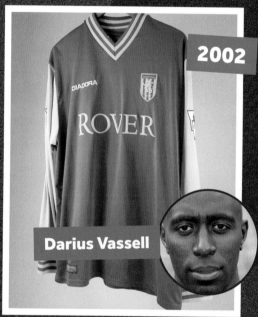

Darius Vassell

2006

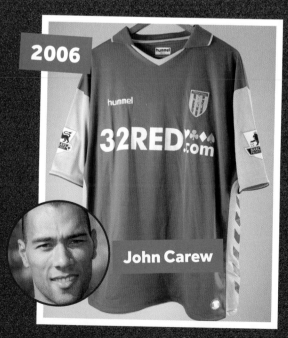

John Carew

2010

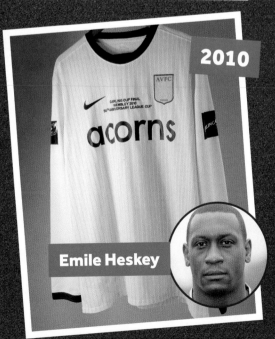

Emile Heskey

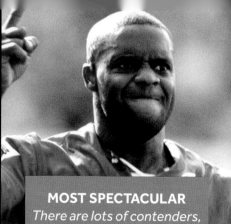

FASTEST
Dwight Yorke headed Villa into the lead after just 13 seconds at Coventry City in 1995 – Villa's fastest Premier League goal. But even that wasn't as fast as Bob Iverson after nine seconds in a 2-0 win against Charlton Athletic in December 1938.

LONGEST
There may have been others from a similar distance in bygone days, but Stiliyan Petrov scored from the centre circle in a 6-0 win at Derby County in 2008.

MOST SPECTACULAR
There are lots of contenders, from long-range volleys to diving headers, but what about Dalian Atkinson's mesmerising run and delicate chip against Wimbledon at Selhurst Park in 1992?

GOLDEN GOALS

Villa have scored many significant goals throughout the course of the club's history. Here are just a few of them...

MOST INTRICATE
Every player except Shaun Teale and keeper Mark Bosnich was involved in an amazing move before a Dwight Yorke tap-in against Sheffield Wednesday in 1993.

LONGEST HEADER
Peter Aldis from 35 yards against Sunderland in 1952. It sounds impossible, and maybe it is – but the full-back's header bounced over the keeper!

MOST CRUCIAL
It must be Peter Withe's European Cup winner in 1982!

VILLA FIRSTS

DEADLY DALIAN

Dalian Atkinson was the first player to score for Villa in the new FA Premier League when it was launched in August 1992. Atkinson netted the equaliser in an opening day 1-1 draw against Ipswich Town at Portman Road – and was also on target in the next two games as Villa drew by the same score against Southampton and Leeds United.

OUR WILLIE

Villa's first black player was Willie Clarke, who signed from non-League Bristol Rovers in the summer of 1901. Although he was born in Scotland, Clarke's father was from British Guiana.

On Christmas Day in 1901, Clarke became the first black player to score in a Football League game, netting in Villa's 3-2 win at Everton.

STAN THE WHAM

Stan Lynn was the first full-back to score a hat-trick in English football's top division. Nicknamed "Stan the Wham", he was on target three times – including two penalties – when Villa beat Sunderland 5-2 in January 1958. Lynn scored a total of 38 goals in 324 games for the club.

THE HIGH SEAS

The club embarked on their first overseas tour in May and June 1926, playing six matches in Sweden, Denmark and Norway. They travelled by ship, and a few players suffered from sea-sickness – which is possibly why they lost the first two games! At least they won the other four.

PENALTY KING

The first time Villa were involved in a penalty shoot-out was in September 1979. After beating Colchester United 2-0 away in a second-round League Cup tie, Ron Saunders' men lost by the same score at Villa Park in the second leg. Extra-time failed to produce any further goals, so the game was settled by a shoot-out, Tony Morley converting the final kick to give Villa a 9-8 victory.

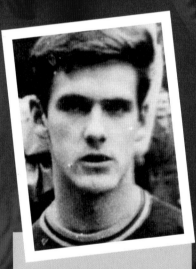

DEAN'S HAT-TRICK

Villa's first Premier League hat-trick was scored by Dean Saunders. The Wales international, a club record £2.3million signing from Liverpool, netted three times – including two penalties – as Ron Atkinson's side thrashed Swindon Town 5-0 at home in February 1994.

SUPER SUB

Midfielder Graham Parker was Villa's first replacement when substitutes were introduced to football at the start of the 1965-66 season. Initially, just one sub was allowed, although it was the tenth game of the season before manager Dick Taylor made a switch, sending on Parker to replace striker Tony Hateley in a 3-2 home victory over Tottenham Hotspur.

OPERATION RESTART

Villa were involved in the first game to be played behind closed doors as part of Operation Restart following the Covid-19 outbreak of 2020. Dean Smith's side drew 0-0 against Sheffield United at Villa Park.

IT MUST BE... IT IS!

Every week we follow the boys in claret and blue.

We even conquered Europe in 1982.

It will be 40 years in May since Aston Villa's finest hour – victory over Bayern Munich in the European Cup final.

The boys were not in claret and blue that night. They wore white shirts with claret pinstripe to avoid clashing with the red of their German opponents.

But none of the 12,000 fans who travelled to Rotterdam – and thousands more watching at home on TV – was worried about that as Peter Withe scored the most important goal in the club's history.

The road to Rotterdam had begun nearly eight months earlier when Villa, having won the League Championship for the

first time in 71 years, kicked off their first European Cup campaign with a comfortable 7-0 stroll against Icelandic part-timers Valur – 5-0 at Villa Park and 2-0 in Reykjavik.

Next up was a much tougher test, against BFC Dynamo. But Tony Morley's two brilliant goals gave Villa a 2-1 first-leg advantage in Berlin and although the East Germans won 1-0 in the return match at Villa Park, Ron Saunders' men went through on the away-goals rule.

By the time of the quarter-final in March, Saunders had resigned and been replaced by Tony Barton, who guided the team to

a 2-0 win against Dynamo Kiev before another fine Morley goal was enough to secure a semi-final victory over Anderlecht.

Then came that unforgettable night in Rotterdam. Barton was forced to make a substitution after only nine minutes when goalkeeper Jimmy Rimmer was forced off with a neck injury. But the inexperienced Nigel Spink made some brilliant saves before Withe's wonderful 67th-minute winner.

As ITV commentator Brian Moore observed: "It must be. And it is. Peter Withe!"

ANSWERS

Player Managers

1. ALEX MASSIE (1945-49)
2. ERIC HOUGHTON (1953-58)
3. VIC CROWE (1970-74)
4. RON ATKINSON (1991-94)
5. BRIAN LITTLE (1994-98)
6. JOHN GREGORY (1998-2002)

*Ron Atkinson never played for the first team

Find the full-backs

1. G I D M A N
2. C H A R L E S
3. S T A U N T O N
4. A I T K E N
5. D E L A N E Y
6. P R I C E
7. S W A I N
8. G I B S O N
9. W R I G H T

Spot the Ball

The French Connection

S	A	N	S	O	N	A	E	G	L
Y	M	B	M	R	X	J	G	H	N
L	A	U	C	W	D	S	I	X	A
F	V	B	E	R	S	O	N	Q	O
C	I	S	S	O	K	H	O	S	G
H	J	E	Y	N	K	P	L	B	L
I	V	R	D	C	T	W	A	E	I
G	U	I	L	B	E	R	T	Y	A
O	K	P	A	Y	L	Z	B	E	W
J	A	D	A	K	O	D	J	I	A

Name on the shirt

1. WATKINS
2. INGS
3. CASH
4. MINGS
5. KONSA
6. TRAORE
7. DAVIS
8. RAMSEY
9. TARGETT
10. McGINN
11. SANSON
12. TREZEGUET

Do you know Ezri Konsa

1. A – LONDON
2. C – CHARLTON ATHLETIC
3. C – BRENTFORD
4. B – CREWE ALEXANDRA
5. A – EVERTON

Spot the Difference

61